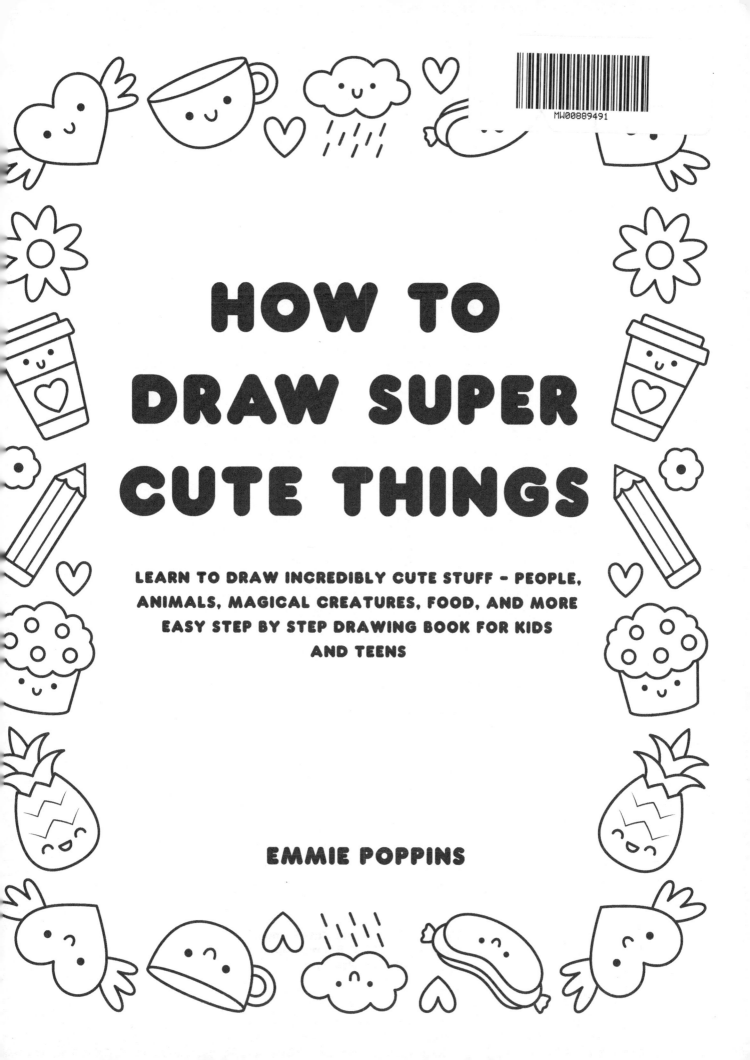

HOW TO DRAW SUPER CUTE THINGS

LEARN TO DRAW INCREDIBLY CUTE STUFF – PEOPLE,
ANIMALS, MAGICAL CREATURES, FOOD, AND MORE
EASY STEP BY STEP DRAWING BOOK FOR KIDS
AND TEENS

EMMIE POPPINS

★ ★ ★ ★ ★

Thank you for buying our book!

If you find this drawing book fun and useful, we would be very grateful if you could post a short review on Amazon! Your support does make a difference and we read every review personally.

If you would like to leave a review, just head on over to this book's Amazon page and click "Write a customer review."

Thank you for your support!

★ ★ ★ ★ ★

CONTENTS

LET'S LEARN THE BASICS!

CHIBI - CUTE PEOPLE

CUTE ANIMALS

CUTE MAGICAL CREATURES

CUTE ITEMS

CUTE FOODS

INTRODUCTION

This book will teach you how to draw cute things. It's very easy! Just follow the instructions and have fun!

TOOLS THAT YOU CAN USE

Use a pencil and eraser to sketch. Don't forget to sharpen your pencil before you start!

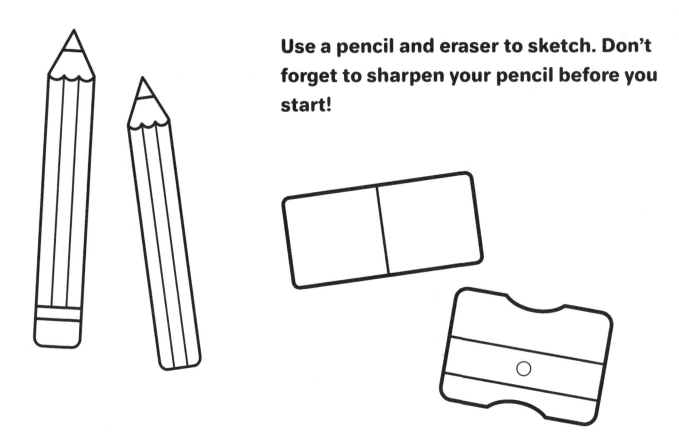

Use different pens and liners to start the outline. You can use a fountain pen, a ballpoint pen, or even a very thin marker.

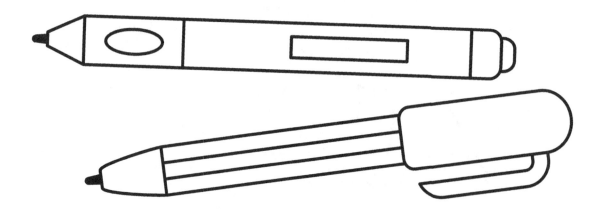

SURFACES

You can draw on whatever you want! Use separate sheets of paper, a notebook, or a sketchbook. You can choose tinted paper to make the drawing more interesting, or you can even try drawing with white pens on black paper!

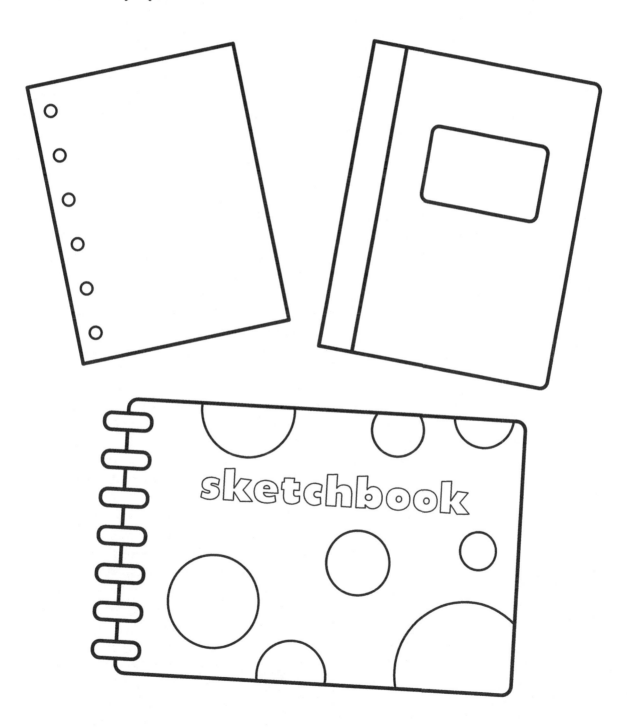

LET'S LEARN
THE BASICS!

THE BASICS OF DRAWING CUTE THINGS

Let's take a look at the most important aspects of all things cute.

First of all, you need to draw in a simple style. Don't overcomplicate it! Simplify the overall silhouette and skip the unnecessary details. All the corners must be rounded to keep your figure looking soft and playful. Sharp edges just aren't on the theme!

Faces make things even cuter. Look at this cute cup of coffee, for example. A caffeinated beverage has never looked more adorable!

ANYONE CAN DO IT!

**Don't doubt your abilities!
Everyone can draw cute things!**

You don't need to know anatomy or any complicated artistic techniques. Realism isn't the goal. What you want to do is distort the shape of your figure so that it's plump and rounded. Use circles and ovals to create the shape.

Try to draw distinctive features so that the character is recognizable. Look at this cute bunny, for example. He certainly doesn't look like a real rabbit, does he? But his ears and teeth give it away. Simplifying your figures to their main characteristics is the first step.

EYES

Let's face it, cuteness begins with the eyes! So, let's learn how to draw the most expressive features on our figure's little face.

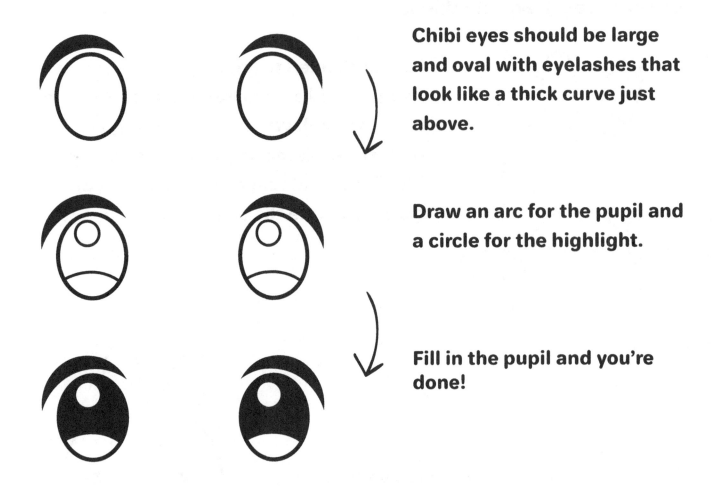

Chibi eyes should be large and oval with eyelashes that look like a thick curve just above.

Draw an arc for the pupil and a circle for the highlight.

Fill in the pupil and you're done!

The eyes of animals and objects can be simpler. You can choose whether to include highlights or not in round eyes. You can also draw the eyes as arcs or lines to represent emotions.

MOUTH

Let's learn how to draw a mouth!

 A chibi should have a wide mouth. It may be in the shape of a curved oval with an arc inside to represent the tongue.

 The mouth may also be in the form of a semicircle with a curved top.

 When drawing a chibi animal, the upper part of the mouth could consist of two curves to represent the philtrum in its upper lip, which is seen on cats and many other mammals.

 Use a simple arc to draw a cute smile.

The mouths of the subjects should look like simple semicircles and arcs. Use two connected arcs to draw the mouth of some of the animals.

SHADOWS

You can use shadows to add volume to your characters. First, decide which side the lighting will be on. You should draw a shadow on the opposite side.

Light

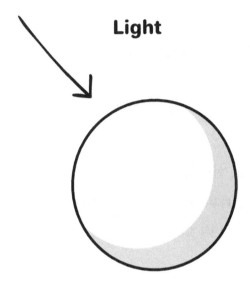

The shadow should follow the outline of the character. In the example below, the figure's wavy hair in the background is a little darker to create some depth.

CHIBI - CUTE
PEOPLE

HOW TO DRAW CUTE PEOPLE

1. Proportions

The human figure consists of two full circles and approximately one-tenth of a circle in height. The body should be oval and equal to half the top circle in width.

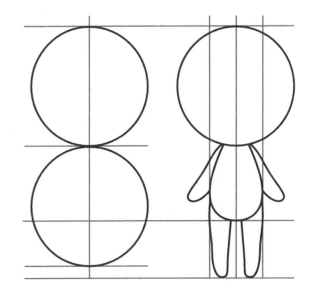

2. Perspective

Use a vertical midline and a horizontal eye line. If you lower the line of the eyes downwards, your character will look down. If you raise it, they'll look up. If you move the lines to the side, your character will be turned in that direction. Note that the far eye, arm, and leg should be slightly higher.

3. Simple and cute style

The face should be composed of simple shapes.

All parts of the body should be simplified and plump. Draw the arms and legs short to make the character cuter.

4. Hairstyles

You can draw a hairstyle of any length and shape. Just use puffy and rounded shapes to fit with the overall soft and plump composition of the figure.

5. Accessories

You can add bows, sweets, animal ears, and other delightful elements to show the character's personality.

ACCESSORIES

You can add various accessories and effects to show off your character's individuality.

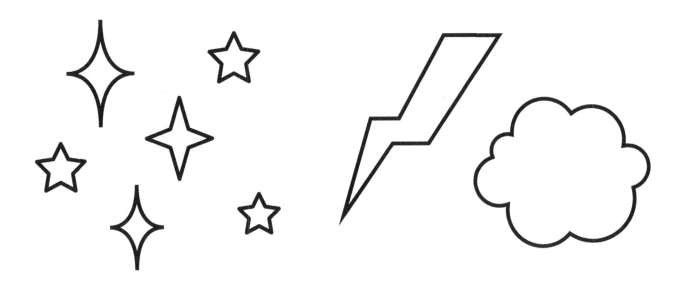

It can be glitter and stars to add magic. You can draw lightning bolts around the character to show its cheeky nature or draw clouds around the chibi who's known to be a dreamer.

You can add devil or angel wings to the appropriate characters. Chibis with animal personas could have ears and tails. Add bows, sweets, flowers, and hearts to help your characters express themselves!

CHIBI GIRL

1. **Let's draw a cute chibi girl with long hair. Start with a big, round head and a little oval body. Add arms and legs. They should be small and plump, so your chibi will look sweet and unimposing.**

2. **Draw a vertical line in the middle and a horizontal line in the lower third of the oval. Sketch out the face at the bottom half of the head.**

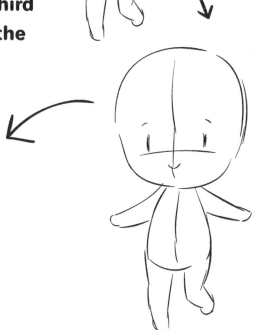

3. **Now comes the fun part! Sketch the clothes and hair. We'll make the skirt wide and pleated. The hair will be very long, almost the full length of the chibi's little body.**

4. Next, you can add your details. First, add curls or bangs to cover part of the face. Then, add big, round eyes and a smiling mouth. Draw a cute little bowtie, or some other accessory, and clothes. Your chibi is almost ready! All you have to do is add arms, legs, and the rest of her hair.

CHIBI BOY

1. The next character is a boy! Start by drawing a large, round head and a small, oval torso. Then, add arms and legs. Don't forget that all parts of the body should be small in relation to the head.

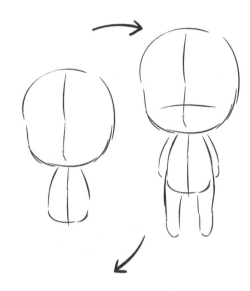

2. Good job! Now draw a vertical line in the middle and a horizontal line in the lower third of the head. Mark the area for the mouth and eyes.

3. Draw the face and hair, and don't forget the ears! Let's dress our chibi in some dashing suspender pants and a t-shirt.

4. Now you can outline your sketch. Start with the face and hair. Then, draw the clothes, arms, and legs. Add boots and cute socks. Our chibi boy is ready!

CHIBI IN A LONG SWEATER

1. Start the drawing by sketching the figure. Make her head noticeably larger than her body. Her arms and legs should be symmetrical.

2. Draw a vertical line in the middle and a horizontal line in the lower third of the oval. Sketch out her face at the bottom half of her head.

3. Now, sketch her hair, eyes, and clothes. The sweater should be long, with sleeves that completely cover her arms.

4. Let's move on to the details. Start with her hair and face. Then, you can draw her sweater. Add cuffs to the sleeves and a zigzag pattern to the fabric. Note that the pattern on the sleeves is slightly shifted upwards. This helps us to separate the sleeves from the body visually. Draw the legs and add round pom poms to the knee socks. Finish the hair and you're done!

BOY IN A SUIT

1. First, draw a sketch of the boy. Note that the chibi is turned a little and we can see his left side more than the right. Divide his head into three parts with two vertical lines. The left line will be the middle line of the figure.

2. The boy's hair can be a little disheveled in this example. Draw the costume and don't forget that the chibi is turned to his right, with his left side facing us. So, the right side of the suit will be narrower, and we will only see a small part of his right arm. Good job!

17

3. Now, you can start your line drawing! Draw his tousled hair and smiling face. All you have to do is add an outfit and voila! Our suited chibi is ready. Looking snazzy!

CHIBI BEE

1. Chibi in a bee costume? Chibi in a bee costume! First, sketch out the figure. This chibi is running at an angle, which means that the vertical axis of the figure should be tilted to the left.

2. Sketch out her eyes and smiling mouth. Remember that her facial features should be tilted too.

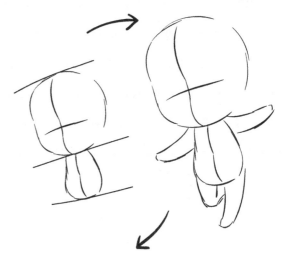

3. Now let's make the costume. It should be a hoodie with wings and funny bee antennae. A few strands of hair could peek out of the hood as well to add a bit of character.

4. Start tracing your sketch from the hood downwards. Then, add her face before completing the costume. Let's give her simple pants and high boots on her feet. Now, the most important details! Add antennae, wings, and bee stripes. You're done! She's looking as cute as can bee!

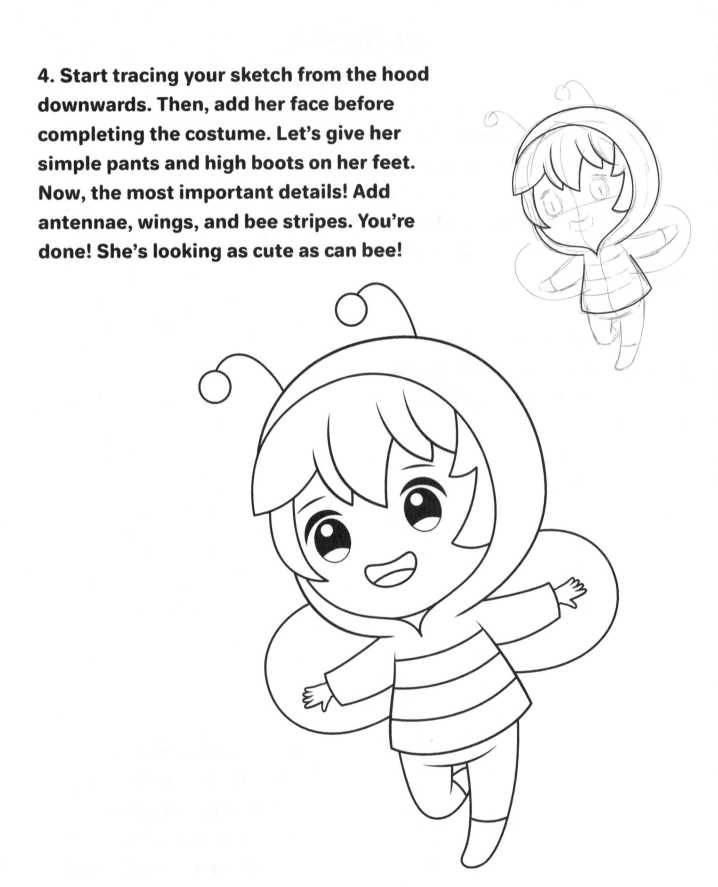

DEVIL CHIBI

1. How about a cute little devil? Sketch out his head and torso first. The boy should stand straight with his arms crossed over his chest.

2. Sketch the face and note that it should be symmetrical. Perfecto!

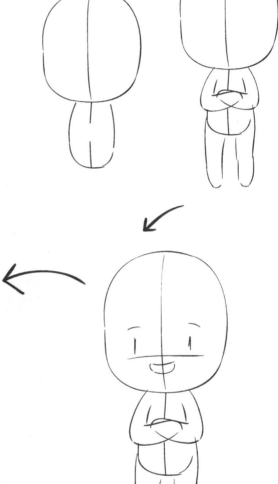

3. Draw his luscious locks and a long coat. Let's give him simple trousers to wear and some stylish boots. Now draw his cute little wings, horns, and tail.

4. Let's proceed to the final touches. Start with his head and then add the outfit. Don't forget to draw the devil elements. Our chibi is ready and looking sinfully cute!

22

HAPPY CHIBI

1. **Now we will draw a joyful chibi in a ruffled dress! Our figure is in motion, so sketch her leaning to the left with her arms raised. Turn her left leg to the side so she doesn't topple over!**

2. **Her head will be tilted back slightly, so you should draw her eyes and mouth a little higher than usual.**

3. **Draw long hair and let bangs fall over her face. Add a puffy, two-layered dress with ruffles. Stunning!**

4. Now draw the hair, a happy, smiling face, and a dress. Let's add ruffles to the sleeves and a cute collar. Don't forget to add the little shoes. Our happy chibi is ready!

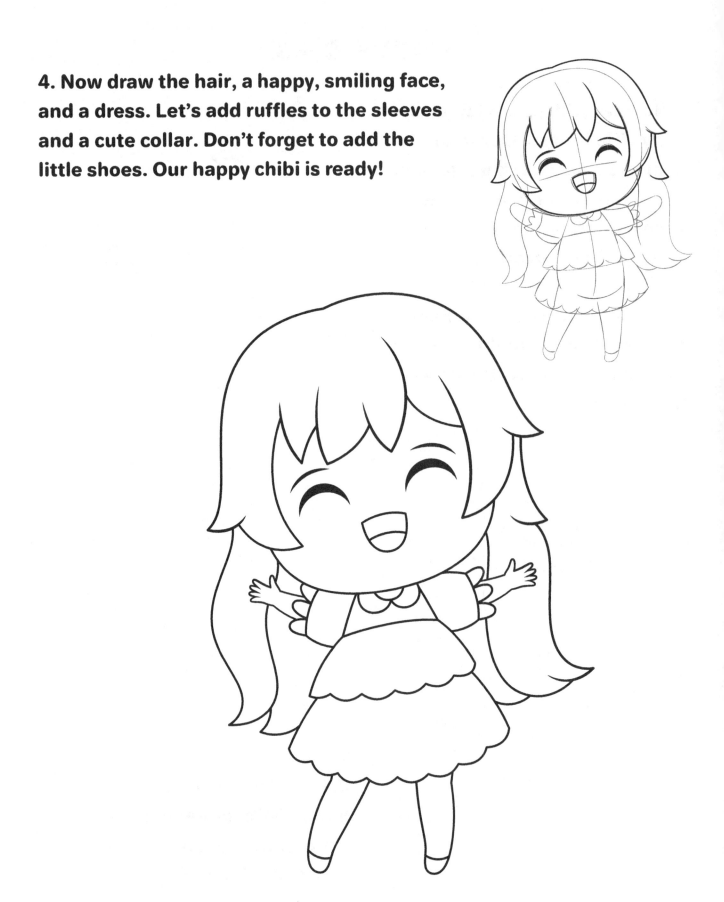

CHIBI CAT

1. Let's draw a cute, cat-eared chibi! Draw a figure turned slightly to the left this time. The median line should be shifted to the left, as well as his arms and legs.

2. Draw a horizontal line in the lower third of the oval, and sketch out the face at the bottom half of the head.

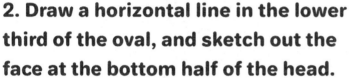

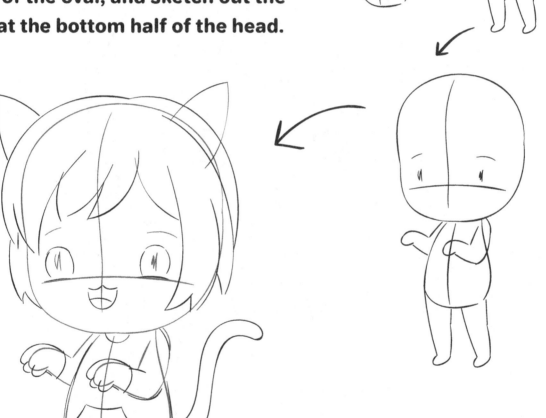

3. Now the fun part! Add shaggy hair, cat ears, and a face. Note that the mouth looks like a cat's. Draw his puffy jumpsuit with a tail. Your chibi is looking *purrfect*!

4. Last but not least, you can outline your sketch. Start with his head and smiling face. Then, move on to the costume. Note that his mittens should look like a cat's paws. Voila! Your cat-eared chibi is ready!

SWEET CHIBI

1. Now, let's draw a candy-themed chibi! Start by sketching her head and torso. This time, our figure will stand straight and be symmetrical on either side.

2. Draw a vertical line in the middle and a horizontal line in the lower third of the oval. Sketch out the face at the bottom half of the head.

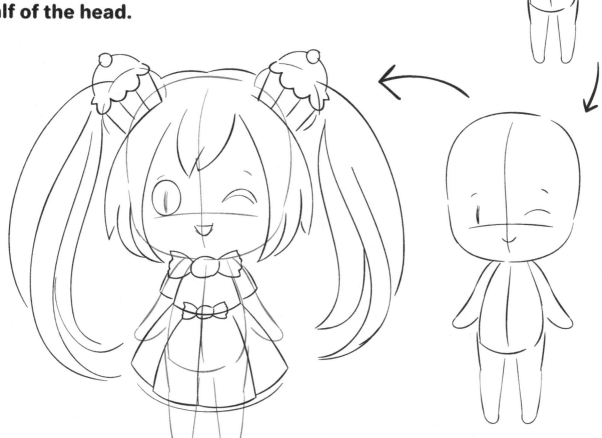

3. Now, draw cupcakes on her head and add long ponytails. We'll draw one of her eyes closed to make it seem as if she's giving us a cheeky wink. Add a puffy dress with various candies. Looking sweet!

4. We can now outline her dress and add her candy accessories. We'll place her hands behind her dress and add some adorable pom-poms to her shoes. She's as sweet as can be!

CHIBI FOX

1. Let's draw a happy, fox-eared chibi next! Start with a figure tilted to the left to create the impression of movement. Her left hand can be raised in a friendly wave.

2. The face should also be tilted. Sketch out her eyes and smiling mouth. Perfect!

3. Now add her hair, fox ears, and round eyes. Draw a big bow on her chest and then add the outfit. Once you've added the tail, you can move on to the main drawing.

4. First, draw a fringe covering part of the face. Then, add big, round eyes and a smiling mouth. We'll also give her a pair of giant, adorable fox ears! Keep her arms and legs short and chubby to make her proportions cutesy. Finally, draw a big, fluffy tail and you're done!

CUTE ANIMALS

HOW TO DRAW CUTE ANIMALS

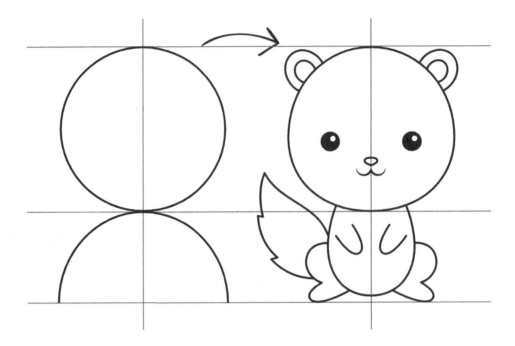

To create cutesy proportions, we'll give our animal a large head and a tiny body. For the height of the animal, we can draw one and a half circles of equal size. The top circle can be used as the head, while the body can be drawn in place of the half-circle below. Draw short, chubby paws to make your little critter even cuter.

Shift the median line and draw the animal turned to the side. The muzzle and other parts of the body should be tilted to ensure that the entire figure is facing the same direction.

LLAMA

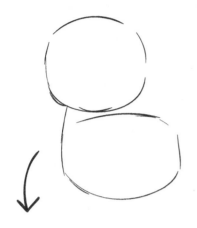

1. I hope you're ready to draw an incredibly cute animal! It's llama time! Start with two ovals. The head should be slightly rounder and the body a tad elongated.

2. The llama's neck and legs should be short and plump. We're keeping it cutesy, as always! Next, mark a place for the muzzle.

3. Draw fluffy, cloud-like fur along the whole body. There should be no fur on the muzzle, so the curls around it should be directed inward. Finally, add a tail, ears, and hooves to the drawing.

4. Look at the stunning sketch you've made! Now we just need to outline it. Draw the curly fur on the body of the llama. Then, a muzzle and other details. No *probllama*!

DOG

1. Draw two ovals, as shown in the picture. These will guide you when you draw the doggy's head. Next, add an oval for the body below. Outline a pair of oval ears, thick paws, and a shaggy tail.

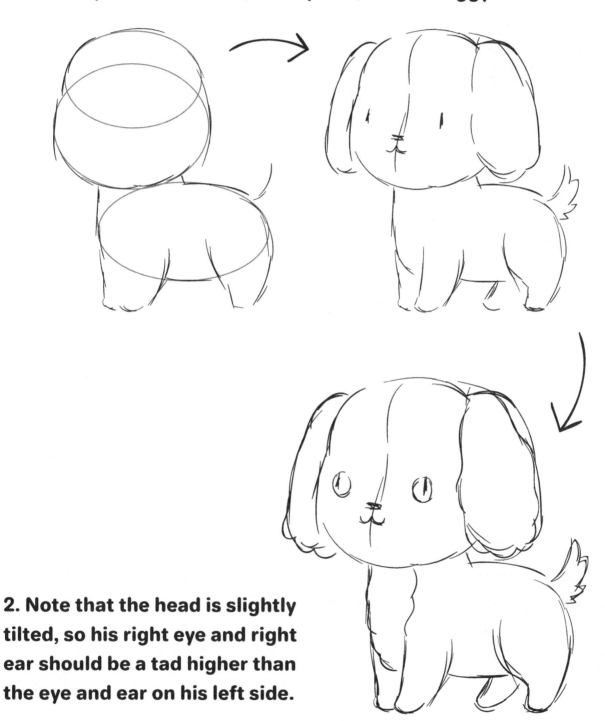

2. Note that the head is slightly tilted, so his right eye and right ear should be a tad higher than the eye and ear on his left side.

3. Now, we can finalize our outlines and features. Add a cute little muzzle on the bottom half of the head. We can also add some wavy fur on the chest and ears. *Paws-itively* adorable!

FOX

1. The fox should have an elongated head and large ears. We can then add a small body and chubby paws. The median line of the head should be shifted to the left here so we can get a good look at his hind legs and tail.

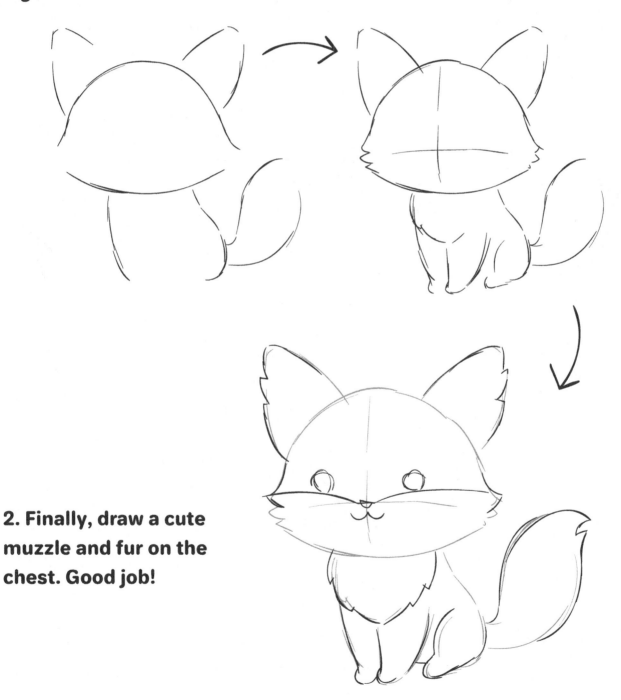

2. Finally, draw a cute muzzle and fur on the chest. Good job!

3. Now you can trace the sketch and add a few details, for example, a zigzagged stripe to the tail to indicate the white tip. Don't forget to draw the inside of the ears. What a cute little fox!

PANDA

1. For our adorable little panda, let's start with an oval body and a big head. The median line can be shifted to the left once again.

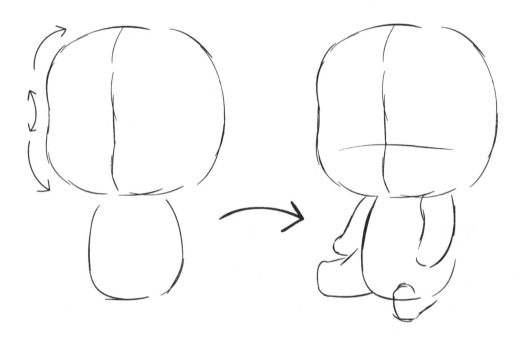

2. This panda should have round ears and thick paws. One hind paw will be directed forward and the other will be turned to the side, as seen below.

3. Now you can outline the sketch. Next, draw the muzzle and add ovals around the eyes. Add some paw pads for an extra little detail and then you're done!

MOUSE

1. Time to try a mouse! Sketch the head and body, as per usual. The shape of the head is a circle slightly expanding at the bottom. The mouse should have large, round ears. Note, once again, that the head is tilted.

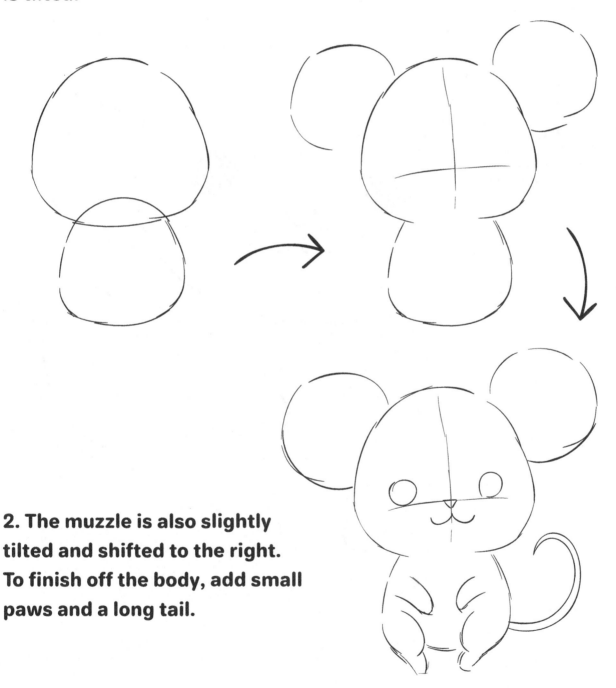

2. The muzzle is also slightly tilted and shifted to the right. To finish off the body, add small paws and a long tail.

3. Now outline your sketch and add the inner part of the ears. Good job! No mouse pun this time. They're too cheesy.

BUNNY

1. For our bunny drawing, we'll start with a circle for the head that expands a little at the bottom. Note that the head is tilted again. We can then add the small body. The bunny is turned to the right this time, so the median line should be shifted to the right.

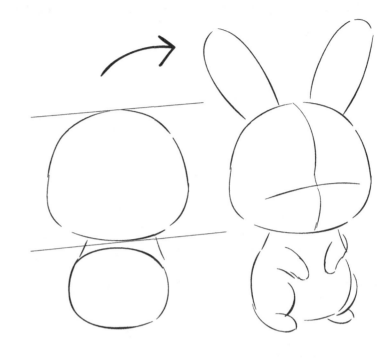

2. Our bunny shall have a bewitching pair of fluffy ears and some adorable little paws to boot. His round little belly can partially cover his right hind leg. He is a cute little chubster, after all! Finally, draw a muzzle and a round tail. Excellent work!

3. Finally, outline your sketch. Add the inner part of the ears and draw his fluffy tail. Add two big teeth and you're done! Now, we can hop along to the next drawing.

PENGUIN

1. Our penguin's body will be made of two connected ovals. We can then add two raised flippers, as this is a very cheery penguin.

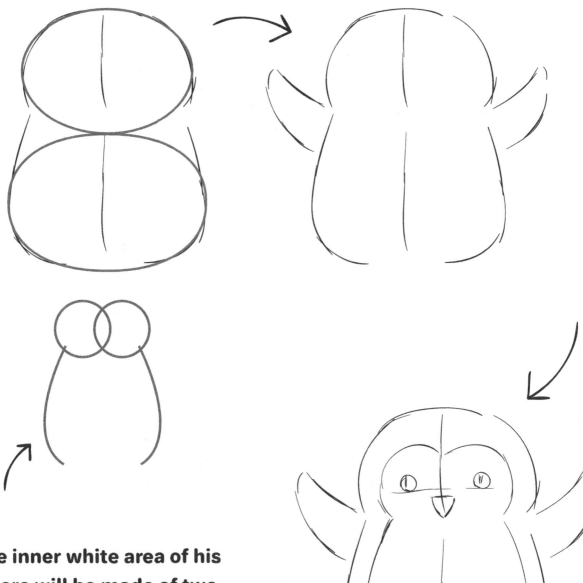

2. The inner white area of his feathers will be made of two circles and two arcs. Add a triangular beak, eyes, and two little feet. All done!

3. You've made a beautiful sketch! All you need to do now is outline it. Good job!

KOALA

1. Now for a koala! First, draw the trunk of a tree leaning to the left for the little guy to grip onto. Then, add a big round head and a small oval body. The head should be tilted, and the median line should be shifted to the left. Perfect!

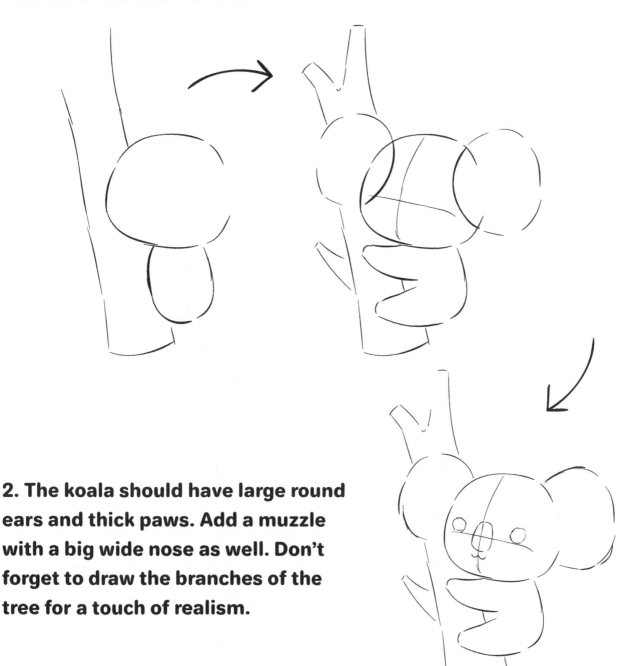

2. The koala should have large round ears and thick paws. Add a muzzle with a big wide nose as well. Don't forget to draw the branches of the tree for a touch of realism.

3. Now you can proceed to the main drawing. Koala ears should be shaggy both outside and inside. Add some leaves to the tree and you're done! Does this koalafy as a pun?

FROG

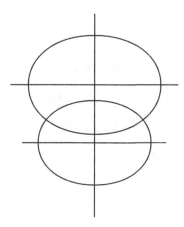

1. He's one kiss away from being a handsome prince! Let's start His Majesty's sketch with two ovals for his head and body. The one for his head should be a tad bigger.

2. Add two circles for his eyes and draw the outlines for his front legs. Then, draw arcs behind him for his hind legs. Dashing!

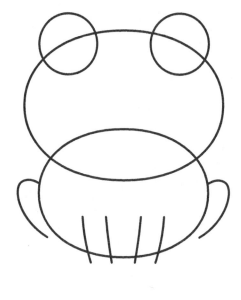

3. Now, proceed with the main drawing. First, complete the front feet using wavy lines to represent his little, webbed toes. Connect two ovals and circles and then finish the hind legs. Add a cute face and you're done!

SLOTH

1. Now for a tranquil sloth. Sketch out a branch for her to hang on to, and then draw two ovals for her head and body. Note that the head should be the same size as the body this time! Add two chubby paws, since we can only see her right ride. Good job!

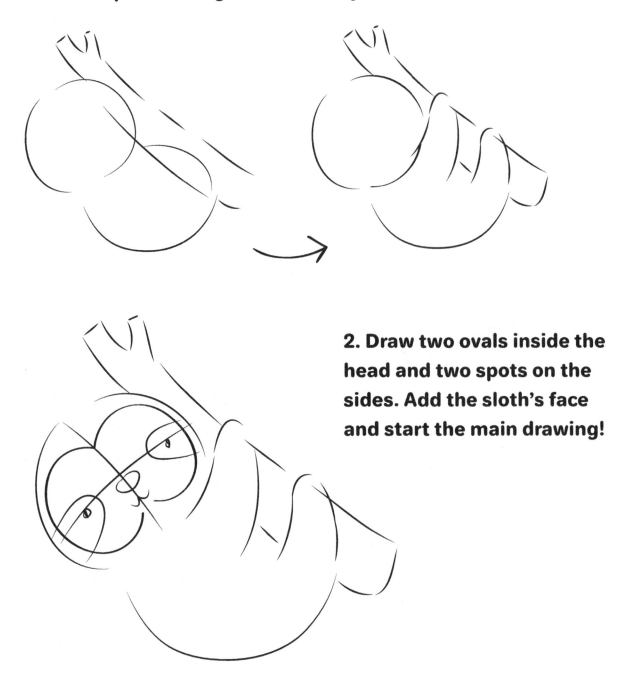

2. Draw two ovals inside the head and two spots on the sides. Add the sloth's face and start the main drawing!

3. Start tracing the sketch. You can start with the head and the adorable face. Then, draw a chubby body and paws. Finally, add a branch with a few leaves for detail. You're allowed to take things slow this time – it's a sloth, after all!

CUTE MAGICAL CREATURES

HOW TO DRAW MAGICAL CREATURES

Let's learn how to draw some magical creatures. We can use an ordinary animal or person as a basis and then add magical characteristics and details.

For example, to draw a unicorn, we use a horse as a basis.

We then add the horn and wings to turn the horse into a unicorn.

This mermaid is a chibi with a long fishtail.

The dragon and dog have the same head shape, but adding horns and some slightly altered features makes all the difference! It's easy, so you shouldn't get too burnt out.

DINOSAUR

1. Who ever thought a giant, carnivorous reptile could be so endearing? For our dinosaur drawing, start with two ovals for the head and one oval for the belly. Then, connect the ovals with smooth lines and draw a short tail on the right.

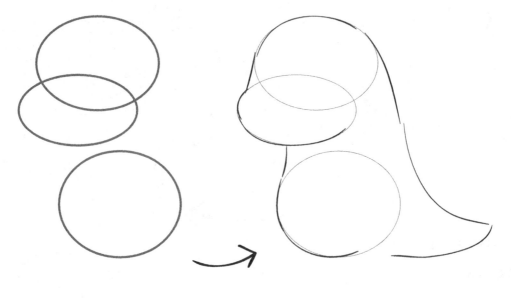

2. Give the dinosaur short, chubby legs, and add a smile. Mark a line for the eyes. Note that his cute muzzle should be slightly tilted, so his right eye and tooth should be higher than the left. Jurassic, I mean, fantastic!

3. Next, draw a pair of round eyes, nostrils, and two pointy teeth. Add a curved line under his left paw to separate the scales on his belly. Lastly, draw rounded ridges on his back and you're done! He looks so sweet and polite; you could almost be tempted to invite him over for tea (rex)!

NARWHAL

1. Now for an existing but equally magical animal – the narwhal! Draw a circle for the head and a line for the end of the tail to start.

2. Then, add two arcs for the tail and connect them to the circle.

3. Finish the tail and add the deadly, adorable horn. Then, draw the fins and a line for the eyes. Notice that the tail, fins, and eyes seem to be directed to the same point on the right. Get it? Point? It's a whale with a horn!

4. Give the narwhal round eyes and a smiling mouth. Finally, draw an oval belly and you're done!

UNICORN

1. For our unicorn drawing, we can start with a circle for the head and an oval for the muzzle. We then connect them using smooth lines. Add an oval body and four chubby legs.

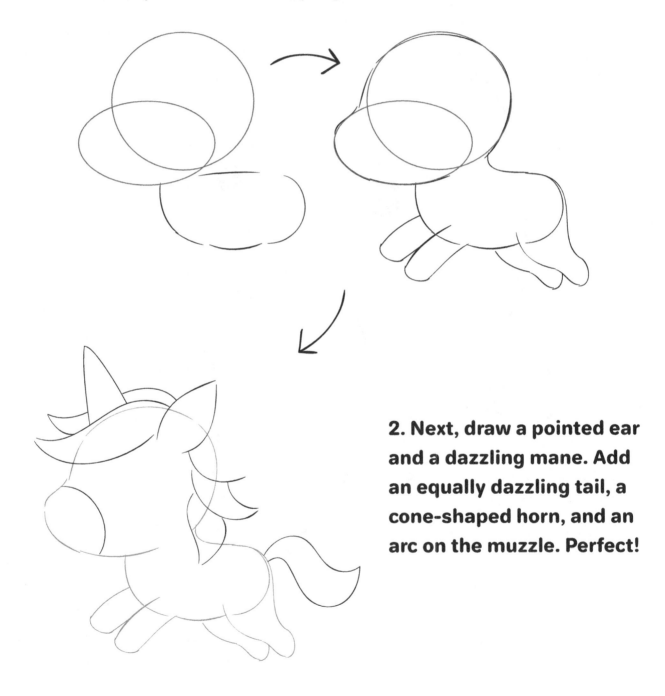

2. Next, draw a pointed ear and a dazzling mane. Add an equally dazzling tail, a cone-shaped horn, and an arc on the muzzle. Perfect!

3. Now, add a round eye and a smiling mouth. Remember the hooves and the inner part of the ear as well. Next, draw curved lines on the mane and tail to represent the strands of hair. As a final touch, all you have to do is add arcs to the horn. Voila - you're done!

DRAGON

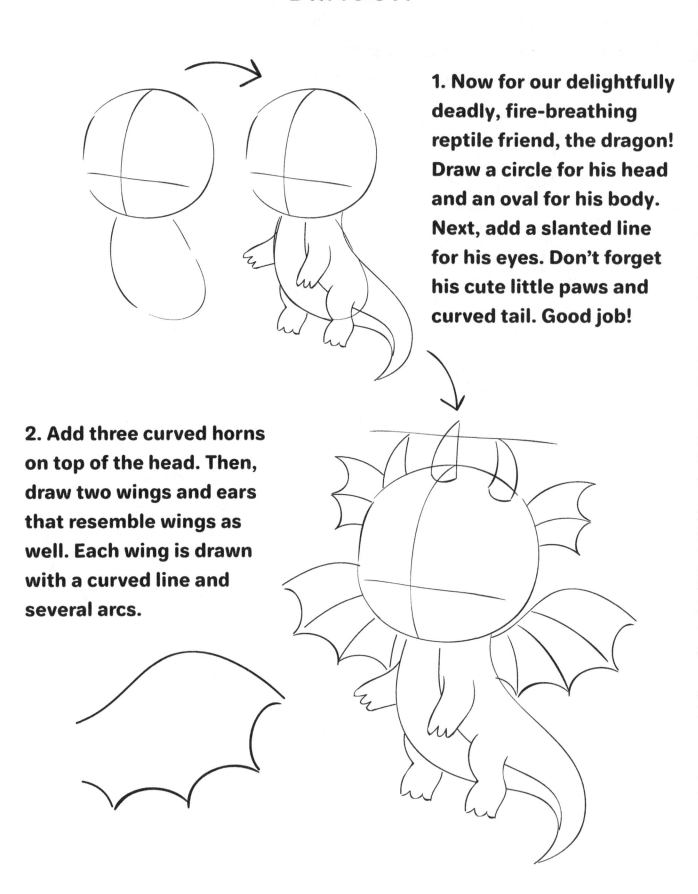

1. Now for our delightfully deadly, fire-breathing reptile friend, the dragon! Draw a circle for his head and an oval for his body. Next, add a slanted line for his eyes. Don't forget his cute little paws and curved tail. Good job!

2. Add three curved horns on top of the head. Then, draw two wings and ears that resemble wings as well. Each wing is drawn with a curved line and several arcs.

3. Lastly, draw the spikes on the tail and a cute muzzle. Your dragon is finally ready to terrorize some unsuspecting, medieval village! Adorbs!

MERMAID

1. Our mermaid should start with a human figure. We begin with a big head and a small body. We then add a curved tail and short arms. The middle line of the figure should be slightly shifted to the left.

2. Draw her curly fringe and a shell-shaped bikini top. Next, give her some gorgeous, wavy locks to brush while sitting on a rock.

3. Finally, outline the sketch, starting with the hair. Add a cute face and some scale details on the tail. And there we are! Our drawing has gone swimmingly!

FAIRY

1. A fairy is another human-like figure, so we'll start by drawing a big head, tilted to the right, and a small body. Then, add short arms and legs. Her left leg should be bent and raised. Note that the fairy figure should be curved to indicate that she's floating. Marvelous!

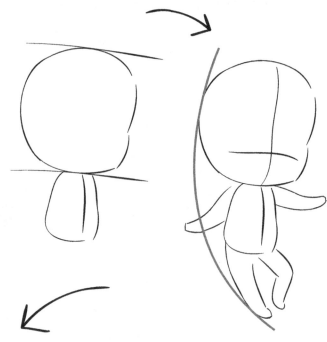

2. We'll give our fairy a stylish, short haircut and cute, pointed ears. Next, draw her dress using curved lines, and then add knee socks. Good job!

3. Now you can proceed to the main drawing. Start with the head and draw her smiling face. Add a large flower and a star on a stick for some detail. Finish drawing the fairy and add the wings behind her back. You've done a magical job!

LEPRECHAUN

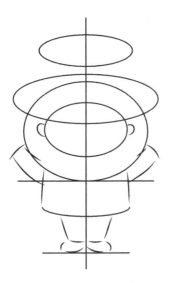

1. To start our leprechaun drawing, we'll sketch two ovals for the hat. Add two more ovals for the head and beard below. Outline the body, legs, and raised arms. Remember, his body parts should be short and plump.

2. Now, let's move on to the main drawing! Draw his beard and face using arcs, and finalize the details for his big, dapper hat.

3. Add a buckle to the hat and a cute bow. Then, draw small plump hands and a cute face. Your leprechaun is ready!

PHOENIX

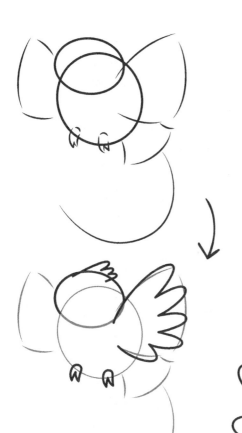

1. For our phoenix, draw two ovals; one small and one large. These will be the head and body respectively. Next, sketch out the wings, legs, and tail using curved lines.

2. Start the main drawing with the wing and then add the crested head. Use curved and oval lines for this. Now, you can draw the talons.

3. Draw a round, plump body, a small beak, and little round eyes. The second wing should be partially hidden behind the body. Next, move on to the tail. Draw the feathered tail using oval and curved lines. Once that's done, your adorable, renewable phoenix will be ready to soar!

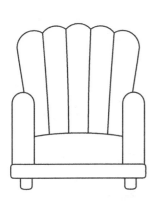

CUTE ITEMS

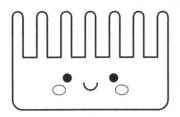

HOW TO DRAW CUTE THINGS

Cute things are made from simple, rounded shapes. Adding faces to ordinary, everyday objects has the interesting effect of making them absolutely enchanting.

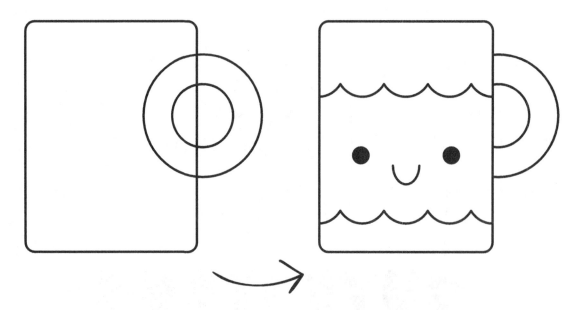

For example, this mug is made from just a rounded rectangle and two circles. Its wonderful, smiling face and simple pattern made from semicircles transforms it into an adorable creature.

There are many different faces that you can use on your objects.

FURNITURE

Let's draw some cute furniture!
Remember: the main idea is that all of our shapes should be round and plump.

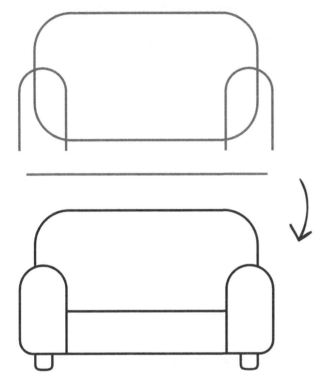

1. Use three rectangles with rounded corners to create the sofa. Now, draw the bottom with rounded corners, and add short legs and a seated line. Ready!

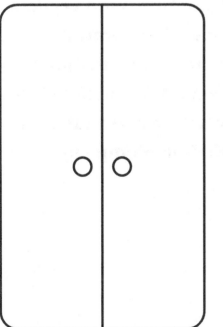

2. The wardrobe is just a rounded rectangle. Draw a vertical line in the middle and round handles on either side.

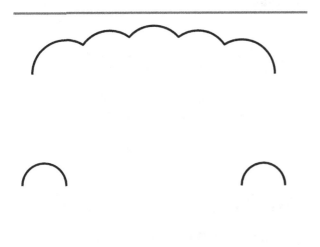

3. Draw a rounded rectangle and two half circles for the chair. Then, add the top of the back, which consists of five connected semicircles.

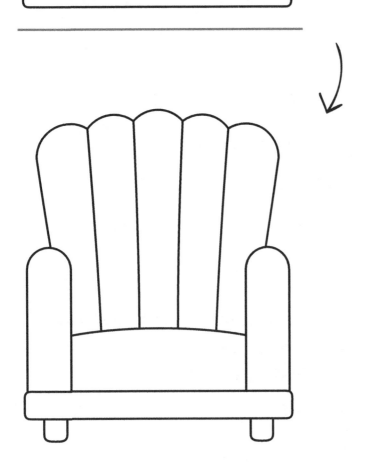

Connect the semicircles to the bottom with vertical lines. Then, draw an arc for the seat. Finally, connect the back to the armrests and seat, and add two plump legs.

CUP

Now, let's draw a cute cup!

1. First, draw an oval. Then, add a semicircle under the oval. It can be more elongated or flatter.

2. Now, add a round handle. Once again, it can be completely round or oval in shape.

3. Draw round eyes and a smiling mouth. Too cute!

CACTUS

If you haven't felt the temptation to hug a pointy desert plant yet, you're about to! Let's draw a cute cactus! There are many types of cacti, so we'll try a few options.

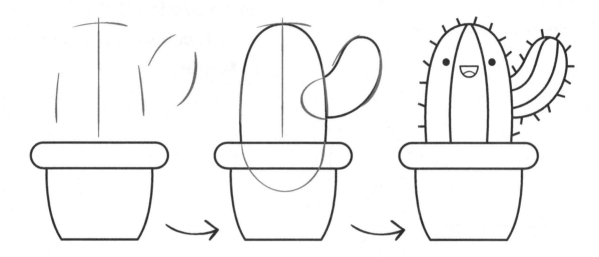

1. First, draw a pot. You can see in the picture below that it will consist of two simple shapes. Then, sketch the cactus. It should be an oval for the main body and a bean-like shape for the offshoot. Add a cute face, spines, and grooves.

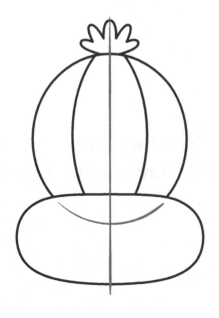

2. The second cactus is very simple. Draw an oval for the pot and a circle for the cactus. Add two grooves and a small flower. This cutie is almost ready!

Now draw the spines and a cute face for each cactus. The spines on the second cactus are made up of three intersecting lines that look vaguely like a star or snowflake. Prickly!

3. For our third cactus, draw a pot in the shape of a trapezoid. Then, add four ovals for the cactus. The ovals should expand slightly at the top.

Give the cactus a smiling face and plenty of prickly spines all over! All you have to do now is add decorative stripes to the pot. Once that's finished, so is your drawing!

PHONE

Do you ever think you might spend too much time staring at your phone? Let's draw one instead!

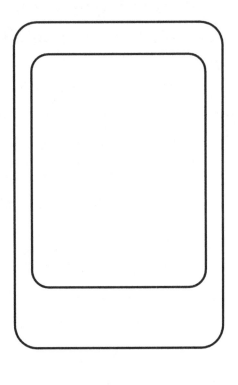

1. Draw two rectangles with rounded corners; one for the phone and one for the screen.

2. Now, add a stripe at the top of the phone and a round button at the bottom. Draw big, round eyes and a smiling mouth. Your cutie is ready to make important calls!

FLOWERS

The only thing better than a flower is a flower with a tiny face.

1. Let's start! For the first flower, draw the bottom of the bud as an oval. There should be three triangular petals at the top. Add a straight stem and two leaves. A pretty flower should have a pretty face!

2. The second flower is made up of a circle and identical oval petals arranged in a circle. Add a curved stem, leaves, and a smiling face. Voila! The flower is ready!

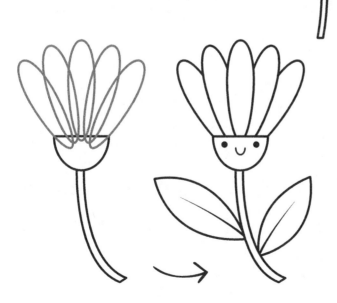

3. For the third flower, start by drawing a semicircle. Then, add oval petals to it. Last bud not least (get it?), draw a stem, leaves, and a cute face. Good job!

CAMERA

Say cheese! Let's draw a cute camera!

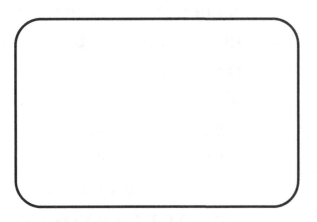

1. First, draw a rectangle with rounded corners.

2. Next, add details to your camera. Don't forget that everything should have rounded shapes to keep the composition gentle and playful. Draw the lens in the form of two circles.

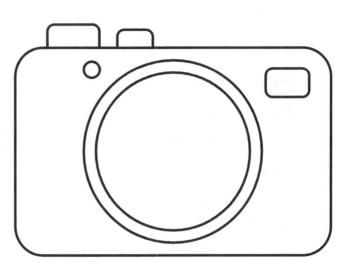

3. Draw a cute, winking face and you're done!

CHRISTMAS TREE

Get festive, everyone. It's time to draw a Christmas tree!

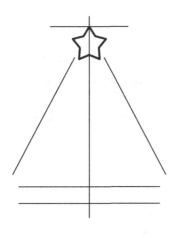

1. Mark the top and bottom of the Christmas tree and the trunk. Draw two slanted lines on the sides to indicate the width of the tree. Then, draw a star at the top.

2. Now, draw three arcs for the crown. The Christmas tree is shaped like a cone, so the arcs should widen towards the bottom. Add another small arc for the trunk.

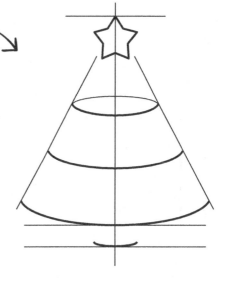

3. Finish the crown by drawing slanted lines from the ends of the arcs. Finish the trunk and add a cute, smiling face. Draw decorations and your adorable Christmas tree is ready!

SCHOOL BUS

What could be cuter than school? Transportation to school, of course!

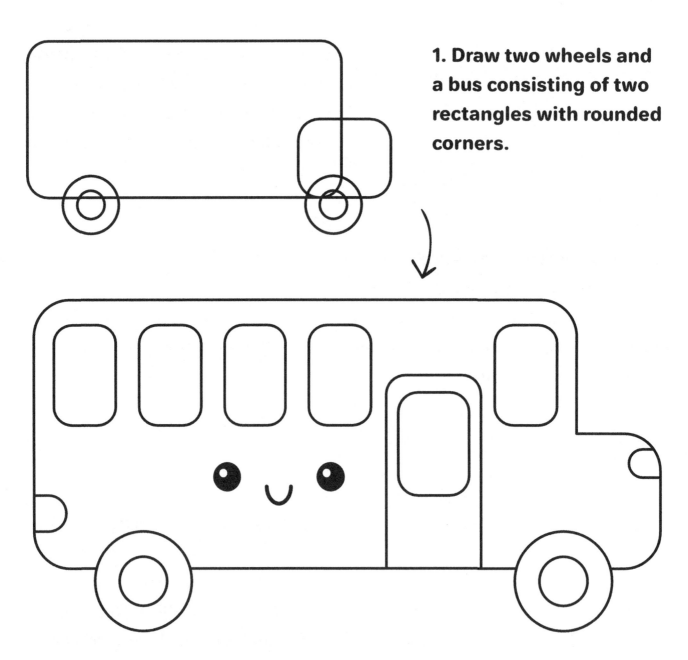

1. Draw two wheels and a bus consisting of two rectangles with rounded corners.

2. Add a door, windows, and two headlights at either end. Don't forget that all your shapes should be rounded. You can then draw a face to make the bus even cuter. You've now arrived at your destination: a finished drawing!

EVERYDAY ITEMS

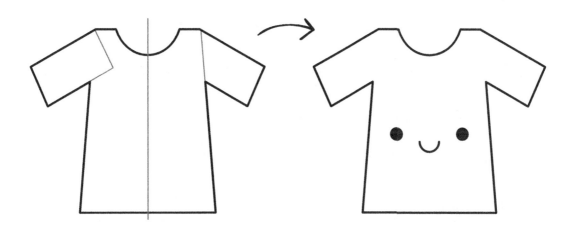

1. The T-shirt is made of a trapeze and rectangular sleeves. Make a round neckline and add a cute face.

2. Draw a rounded rectangle for the satchel and two arcs for the handle. Add two fasteners, a face, and a pocket. Perfect!

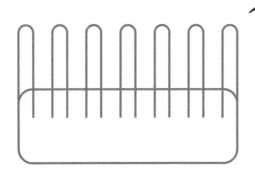

3. The comb is made from a rounded rectangle and several narrow, rounded rectangles. Add a smiley face and you're done!

CUTE FOODS

HOW TO DRAW CUTE FOODS

These adorable food characters are made from simple, rounded shapes. Adding a sweet, smiling face will make them as cute as can be!

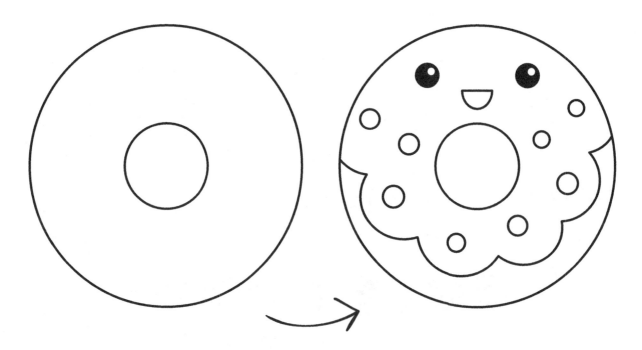

The donut is made up of two circles, one inside the other. The topping is made of half circles and small circles. The donut must have an exceedingly happy face! It's a donut, after all - the happiest of foods.

All the other food characters can mimic how their real-life versions look, but with a simpler and more rounded shape.

POTATO

Let's draw a potato! It's a simple character that is, for whatever reason, quite hilarious.

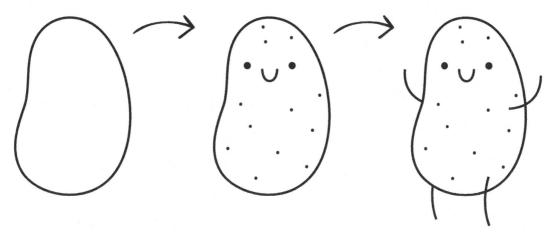

1. First, draw something akin to an oval, but slightly dented in on one side. This will be our potato. Now, you can make your potato character look however you want. For example, you could draw a smiling face and add thin arms and legs. Don't forget to draw some small dots on his body. He's cute, isn't he? And delicious when fried, mashed, or baked.

2. You can draw many different potato characters by changing the face and body position. They are capable of extreme diversity in both art and cooking!

ICE CREAM

You scream, I scream, let's draw some types of ice cream!

1. The first ice cream is made up of a rectangle and a circle. Then, just add a face, a stick, and a wavy topping.

2. For the second ice cream, draw a half circle and some smaller circles surrounding it. This will be the ice cream scoop. Add a cone with a crisscross pattern on it. With the addition of a laughing face, you're done!

3. For the third creamy treat, draw a rectangle and a stick. Add two wavy lines and a face. Then, cut off one corner like someone took a bite for a cheeky detail. Delicious!

FRUITS

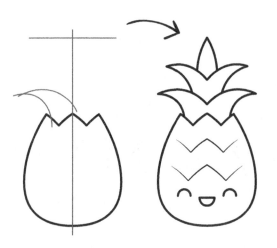

1. The pineapple is made up of an oval that expands downwards with denticles at the top. Add arched leaves, a laughing face, and zigzags to complete it.

2. The apple is made from two oval shapes. It should have a stem and a leaf. Add a face and you're done!

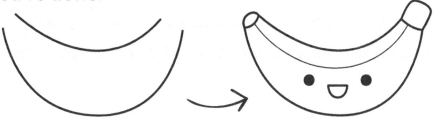

3. Draw two arcs for the banana and then connect them. Note that there should be a ledge on the right. Add a sweet face and details. Perfect!

4. The pear is made of two smoothly connected ovals. There should be a stem and a leaf at the top. Give the pear a happy face as well, so he's not left out!

STRAWBERRY

Now, let's draw a cute strawberry!

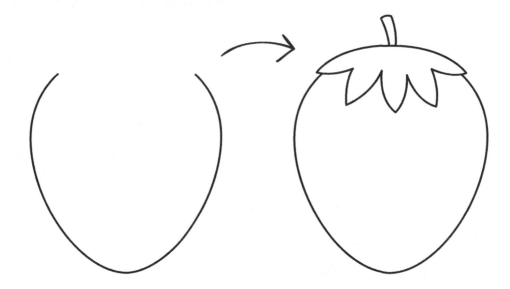

1. The shape of the strawberry is similar to an oval that expands slightly at the top. Add leaves and a small stem to the top of the oval.

2. Draw a cute face and add little seeds. Delectable!

PIZZA

Time for a piece a' pizza!

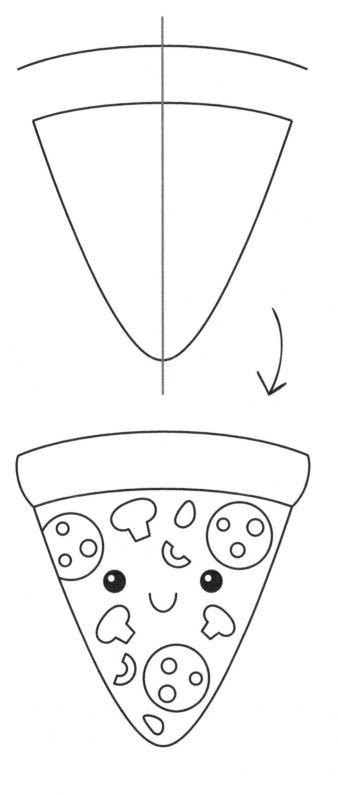

1. Draw two horizontal arcs for the pizza crust and a triangle below. Note that the bottom corner of the triangle is rounded rather than pointed.

2. Draw the sides of the crust with curved lines. Add a cute face and any delicious toppings of your choosing. Scrumptious!

SUSHI

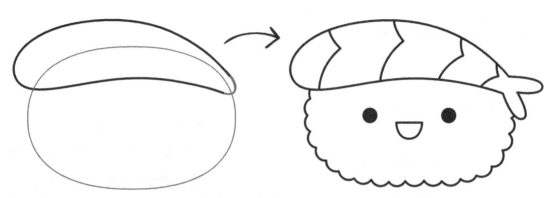

1. For the first piece of sushi, draw an oval for the rice and place the fish on top of it. The fish is made up of a curved, tapering oval. Now, draw the texture of the rice and the smiling face on it.

2. For sushi number two, draw two ovals and connect them to make a nori cylinder. Put the caviar, represented by tiny circles, on the cylinder. Add a face and you're done!

3. For sushi number three, draw an oval for the rice and a curved, narrow oval for the fish. Add a vertical curved stripe. Draw the texture of the rice and the face. Yummy!

CHEESEBURGER

Let's draw this yummy cheeseburger!

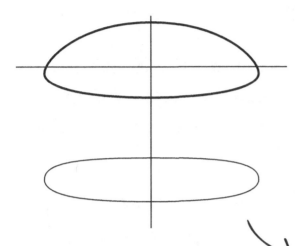

1. Draw the top half of the bun in an oval shape. Note that the oval expands towards the bottom. The top of the oval should be rounder and plumper than the bottom. Sketch an oval for the bottom half of the bun.

2. Now we will draw the filling. Use a wavy line for the lettuce leaf and ovals for the tomato. Then, add curved, rectangular cheese slices.

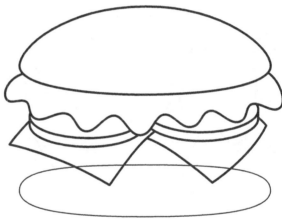

3. Draw a patty using many curved lines. Finally, draw the bottom oval bun and add a cute face. Your cheeseburger is ready! Would you like fries with that?

DONUT

Let's draw some more adorable confections! Donut worry, though - we'll add some new details this time.

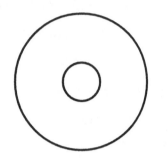

The donut consists of two circles. You can then add different elements, décor, and toppings.

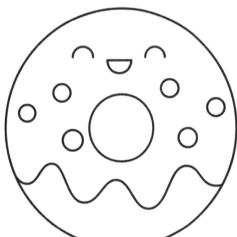

Add a wavy line, circles, and a face to make a cute, simple donut!

Now, try adding ears, horns, a muzzle, and some winding lines. It's a cow donut!

What about ears, a mustachioed muzzle, and a few stripes? Your cat donut is ready! Let's hope it doesn't give you a hairball.

POPCORN

Now for a delicious, salty treat.

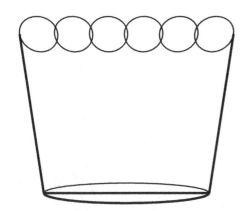

1. Draw a cup tapering down and add a series of small circles to the top. Then, draw vertical stripes that also taper towards the bottom.

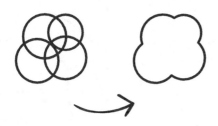

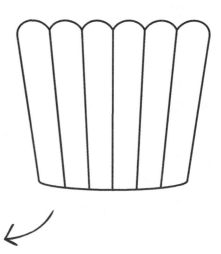

2. Next, erase the side and bottom parts of the circles.

3. Now, draw the popcorn using connected circles. Add a smiley face and your cutie is ready for the movies!

You did an amazing job and can now draw all kinds of kawaii things. Don't stop here! Use these skills to keep developing your creativity and to make cuteness out of the mundane. Thank you for choosing our book!

★ ★ ★ ★ ★

Thank you for buying our book!

If you find this drawing book fun and useful, we would be very grateful if you could post a short review on Amazon! Your support does make a difference and we read every review personally.

If you would like to leave a review, just head on over to this book's Amazon page and click "Write a customer review."

Thank you for your support!

Made in the USA
Las Vegas, NV
18 April 2024

88874250R00063